World Stage Press
Verse from the Village

attuneMEnt

attuneMEnt

poems by
JASMINE BANKS

World Stage Press
Verse from the Village

World Stage Press
Verse from the Village

attuneMEnt
© 2022 Jasmine Banks
ISBN: 978-1-952952-43-2

First Edition, 2022

All rights reserved. No part of this publication may be reproduced, distributed, or transmitted in any form or by any means, including photocopying, recording, or other electronic or mechanical methods, without the prior written permission of the publisher, except in the case of brief quotations embodied in critical reviews and certain other noncommercial uses permitted by copyright law.

Printed in the United States of America

Cover Painting by Sandy Baker-Banks
Cover & Layout Design by Emily Anne Evans

When we are attuned with others, we allow our own internal state to shift, to come to resonate with the inner world of another. My words and poems are dedicated to the people supporting the healing and evolution of our community by unpacking the role that relationships play in our wellness. They are dedicated to the people who do the work to self-reflect and pinpoint the interactions, messages, and experiences that shape the fabric of their intersecting identities and the lens in which they see themselves in the world.

Contents

xiii Foreword

3 Introduction

inception

9 My Inception

10 My Gift

11 10:06pm

13 The Past is Matriarchal, the Future is Femme

15 He Taught Me How to Fish

17 The People's Champ

19 On the Seventh Day

22 The Apple Questions the Tree

24 The Saga Continues

26 Turquoise Staircase

27 Invisible Friend

28 Life

birth

33 My Birth

34 Eat, Prey, Love

36 The Curtains Are Closing

38 All Women?

41 The Root of the Problem

43 Bloodline

44 Another Black Boy Gone

45 Hell, on Earth

47 If You Really Wanna Know

49 Zooming with a Gen Z

51 The "Up-and-Coming" Area

52 So I...

55 Self-Checkout Isn't an Option

57 Us Not Vs.

59 Battle Cry

62 Truth Be Told

growth

67 My Growth

68 This New Year

70 Bread and Butter

72 The Unwritten Oath

74 Out of Office, into Living

76 Medicine Woman

78 May I Have This Dance?

79 Fly a Kite

80 Your Ass is Grass

81 THE Moment

83 Royalty

84 My Favorite Two-Piece

86 Do Not Disturb

87 Slumber Soldier

88 I Take the Reigns

89 The Universe as I See It

91 Acknowledgements

"We delight in the beauty of the butterfly, but rarely admit the changes it has gone through to achieve that beauty."

– Maya Angelou

Foreword
Professor James Douglas Banks, Jasmine's Dad (aka Papa Bear)

My family always instilled in me the need to become educated. One would say that education was something that could not be taken away from you. They also instilled in me the need to work hard in everything that I was involved with on a daily basis. This meant having a high degree of respect for oneself and also for humanity. To this end there were several things I wanted to pass on to my daughter Jasmine as she navigated her path. The first was to study hard. The second was to always do the right thing. The third was to be diligent in your tasks. The fourth was to be intelligent. The final tenet was to be creative. There was also a poem by Langston Hughes which stated,

> "Hold fast to dreams, for if dreams die, life is a broken winged bird, that cannot fly."

This poem I shared with her at a very young age. These were some of the lessons I wanted her to have so that she could fight against the clandestine and overt forces of darkness.

My daughter has carried the torch of a freedom bearer in all aspects of her life. From being a Girl Scout, a regional spelling bee competitor, and a basketball player, she grew into a valedictorian, a USC graduate, ASU master's graduate and now a doctoral student at Loyola Marymount University. She has dedicated her life to address the issues of disenfranchised populations and works within the inner cities of urban America. She has chosen to help those that have been kicked to the curb by society.

There is a strong sense of positivity that comes from her spirit that allows those she encounters to have hope that things will improve in their lives. My daughter could have been successful in other more lucrative areas of economic design, but she chose education because education travels with you on your path.

Our lives are filled with daily encounters that shape our lives and determine our existence.

The following book by Jasmine Banks will take you on her specific life encounters.

It will entail how she dealt with the encounters of family, education, sports, relationships, joy, pain, failure, and success.

While reading this book, you will encounter your own emotional and cognitive reactions to the words on the pages.

The words on these pages might touch you silently or evoke a boisterous response. The words on these pages will lead you to a personal encounter with the author.

As you read through the text, you will not be told what to think, but hopefully it will give you something to think about.

It is my extreme pleasure to introduce my daughter and fellow educator, Jasmine Gabrielle Rose Banks' book, *attuneMEnt*.

attuneMEnt

Introduction

Self-attunement is the ability to access the power of healing, wisdom, and a higher self. It encompasses the capacity to tune into the mind, heart, and body; and thus, tap into the source of energy within you.

My collection of poems explores my own journey of self-attunement. The poems capture my humanity and learning process of my most intimate relationships. I explore how those relationships influenced me and catapulted me to a deeper understanding of myself, including my triggers, needs, desires, and super power of enacting change.

inception

inception:
an act, process, or instance of beginning

My Inception

My family is my origin.
My day sets with their pain.
My sun rises with their love.
They're my compass on Earth
guiding me to what's right.
They move me wisely,
step me up,
make me
great.

My Gift by Sandy Baker-Banks (aka my Mama)

My greatest thought is knowing that you were put here on this Earth for me to know you,
spending time with you, trying to teach you right from wrong,
most of all, to love you.
Although the past few years were very challenging in every way,
you wanting to be you,
me wanting the best for you.
You will be what you've set yourself out to be.
You will be your own accomplishment.
If you live life a true believer,
you'll continue life believing.
If you live life hastily without much regard,
you'll not see too much of life.
I thank God for the gift he has given me in you.
Feelings from within myself give me great happiness just knowing that I've tried.
We will all try during our lives; that's the best we can do.
By the time our lives end, we'll see just how hard we've tried.
Then, and only then, will we see what life was all about.
Be careful in life. Learn from it, respect it, live it to the fullest extent,
always love it and those dearest to you.
Think before you act.
Be you.

Love You Always,
Mama

10:06pm

On the evening of September 1, I bellowed out of the belly of my mother.
The day my cries carved a trail for my voice to take up space.
In those seconds, my forces united.

Virgo synced with the sun,
synthesized my atoms and became the core of who I am.
I am meticulous and intentional with everything I do.

Introspection maximizes the value of my reach,
spanning my arms out to touch minds and hearts,
hugging in the importance of my burrowed purpose.

I have a pressing need to distinguish myself from others,
so I come in hot — speaking, creating, and expressing facts.
You need a cold beverage to counteract the heat that I bring to the table.

Taurus turned in rhythm with my moon,
largely guiding where I want my light to shine.
I create a sense of security and stability for my friends, fam, and lovers.

I often feel powerless to fix messes,
but my practicality and patience make chaos feel manageable.
My loyalty propels me to organize relief for the people I care for.

My moon wanted company so it asked my ascendant to tag along in Taurus.

I am highly attuned to hedonism.
I have a base in reliability and a dash of stubbornness.
I rebel against outdated expectations,
speak my truth and shout it from the mountaintops even if the town is unwilling to hear.
I push against the battalion that attempts to force me to surrender my power.

I enthusiastically turn inwards to inspect the changes that need to happen for my people.
My mouth is blunt. My mind is sharp.
My chart reads DETERMINED.

The Past is Matriarchal, the Future is Femme

My mother protected and soothed me in her womb,
preparing me to harvest my mystique,
preventing the universe from bottling me up.

I escaped her canal and immediately felt the warmth of the matriarchy.
I was born with the heart of a thousand mothers
who raised babies beyond the comfort of their bellies,
nurturing villages even when their uteruses were coated with scars.

Our mothers grew up in a society where women were pressured to remain in the confines of their home,
a dwelling constructed of rickety, rusted nails to hold the discrimination in place,
2x4's that questioned their gifts, muted their hopes, and contested their dreams.

Walls were bursting to tell not-so-far tales,
to shout and share the legacies of our foremothers and the foreshadowing of their baby girls.

I mature with the fire of warriors who course through my veins,
warriors whose conjured up artillery of mental prowess squashes the enemies who campaigned against their worth,
crucified men who weaponized their bodies,
hypnotized foes into recanting allies.

I travel across this murky land with the pulsing spirit of angels.

Emily's attentive ear anticipates the clamor I must extinguish.
Nellie's eyes act as windows of mistakes to learn from.
Rosie's wit gives me the key to trust my intuition.

In my dreams I see their celestial beings, atoms of light
willingly guiding and holding a mirror to me.

In the depths of my darkest hours, Alberta's hands fold in prayer,
Sandy's wizardry tricks me into believing I can survive any day,
Rubina's laughter roars and erases the tears off my cheeks.

I am grateful for the path that is carved for modern women to walk,
blood that built the bricks,
tears that eroded the dirt men threw,
sweat that feverishly dripped well beyond their brows and bosoms
so women today can lead boardrooms in well-conditioned spaces.

The future is femme because of our trailblazers,
our queens who had a fury that rivaled the flames of hell,
fury that sparks the brilliant embers of today,
inspiring consecutive generations to stay ignited.

He Taught Me How to Fish

Study
hard, be diligent,
intelligent, and creative:
an affirming send off at the
juncture of our departures. With one
hand on the wheel, one hand waving
goodbye, he gives me permission to say hello to
a new day of learning. Day upon day, year upon
year, my dad utters these words creating a ripple
effect, surpassing my surface and expanding my self-
worth and pride. Vowels and consonants that he strings
together with the base of his tune unite in my ear
drums, a chorus that speaks power into my being and
releases excellence out of me. My dad, my wiseman
who delivers words that transcend galaxies.
Words he shares with a smile whose
radiance competes with the SoCal
sun. Mahogany cheeks that rival
the yellow star, eclipsing its
shine with his melanin
glow. He encouraged
knobby-kneed Jazzy
to stop conforming to fit
into the sand box, whose frame
refused to let the specs of my gifts
come out and play. He yelled, "cut" during

my
awkward
stage so that my
melancholy Jazz production
couldn't manifest from the printed
screenplay. He dipped me into the
artistic pools of Langston, Maya, and Gil,
leaving Jasmine drenched with the force of our
Black wave makers. When Jas silenced herself, he
let the pen woo me with its glides, acknowledging
my feelings with every droplet of ink. I look upon his
kind eyes framed as storybooks to my soul, stare at his
eyeglasses and see a heroine glaring back at me, an
empowered version of myself in the reflection of his
lenses. In a world where this little Black girl can
feel lost, unseen, and devalued, he taught me...
the hell my voice can raise, the heaven
my words can form, the imprint my
echo can make on this earth for
decades to come. I call
him Papa Bear for
a reason: he takes
pride in raising this
cub; he brought me to
the river and taught me how to
fish, to dip my paws in icy water and
discover a meal I can feast on for years.

The People's Champ

Mama on the right, Life on the left.

Sandra "Acts of Service" Baker-Banks,
born in Upstate New York, bred in Madison, WI,
and flourishing in SoCal.
At an astounding 4 feet 10 inches, this woman packs a mighty punch.

Known as the Gadget Girl,
Little Energizer Bunny,
and Make You Wanna Smack Yo Mama Chef,
she comes to the ring with solutions and well-seasoned meals.

Weighing in at... shhhh, hush your mouth.

Wearing white sneakers found at your local Big 5,
refusing to wear a "brazier" (in her words),

leaving crowds always demanding more,
this dynamic woman has made hundreds of household repairs,
cooked over thousands of meals within a 1600 mile radius,
leaving bellies full and taste buds jumping.

She is not afraid to get her hands dirty in service of others.
You can find her training till the wee hours of the night
clanking her equipment,
perfecting her recipes.

Blasting her Oldies to get in the zone.
You will hear her victoriously singing...
Despite not knowing any song lyrics,
Sandra will hummm and drop a "baabayy" or two.

This powerhouse will knock you off your feet,
twist you into better moods with her fast-talking, ill-humored ways.

She has KO'd lung cancer,
the greatest in short height history,
making her opponents shake to their knees.
The reigning, defending, undefeated, Champion of the World...

My Mamaaaa!!!!

Let's get ready to...

On the Seventh Day

Summers in Slater are unbearable.
Humidity cloaks my skin
like I'm a pig in a blanket
ready to be devoured by the hometown saviors.

Mosquitoes a slangin',
bees a hustlin',
trains a shakin' ,
people a repentin'.

Clock strikes 8,
the countdown begins,
mustering up excuses one by one
until I hear that hum.

Jaazzz??!!

Each letter holding its echo,
bouncing from wall to wall
like the condensation of the sticky air
searching for a place to call home.

Pulling the moist covers back up,
this will be the perfect cover-up.
Barking an inauthentic snore,
doing my best to fully ignore.

Mosquitoes a slangin',
bees a hustlin',

trains a shakin',
people a repentin'.

Very close, very close:
house shoes pressing firmly on the planks,
ushering in new creaks.
I force my eyelids tightly together.

Door swings open.
I huff and I puff away,
tricking into a slumber
trickery doesn't sustain.

Pumpkiiin??!!

A squint, a peak, I try to see.
With one eye open a glimpse is achieved.
There's Granny's muumuu grinning from hip to hip,
stretching floral fabric to a wishful morn.

Mosquitoes a slangin',
bees a hustlin',
trains a shakin',
people a repentin'.

I grunt and give an agreeable mumble.
Granny's pecan cheeks greet her almond eyes,
approving of my nutty behavior
with a nod and the turn of the knob.

Back to sleep I go!

Maybe if I don't get up, she will give up,
give up the hope of repenting my newfound sins
and lack of Baptist buy-in.

Clanking of the jug on the counter,
her orange delight swishes in the cup half full.
Toast is blackened for the umpteenth time.
She scrapes the burnt crumbs,

as I seek to chisel away the uniformity of this town:
country church,
vintage crowd,
a lackluster offering.

Mosquitoes a slangin',
bees a hustlin',
trains a shakin',
people a repentin'.

Granny keeps on,
wakes me every seventh day.
Forever in the creases of my brain waves
and at the tip of her tongue...

Bless your heart

Apple Questions the Tree

Curses, fuck you's, all the insults.
Silence, rejection catapult.

FUCKIN' STUPID!

Mama and Daddy are at it.
Fighting has become a habit.

(DOORS SLAM)

Curly baby criss-crossed, perked eyes.
Wondering why she solely cries.

Confusion now mirrors actions.
Raised to believe harm is passion.

Lashes out with a razor tongue
anytime she feels her heart's stung.

Closes doors without a second thought,
fulfilling the role she was taught.

26 with unlearned lessons,
forced to ask all the hard questions:

Why can't she express her feelings?
Popping off won't lead to healing.

Why does she always run away?
Pain cements a dead-end one-way.

Will she break this ramped cycle?
Hey, generational spiral!

The Saga Continues

I've dreaded losing you for 8,030 days.

A paranoia that paralyzes me the way
    your unhealthy choices cripple your ability to live.

A simple unanswered call puts me into a tailspin.
Unable to function until your well-being is cleared.

I've dreaded losing you for 192,720 hours.

Lips laced with grease,
veins pulsing with glucose,
heart attack.

Smokey airways,
resting tumors,
lung collapse.

I've dreaded losing you for 11,503,200 minutes.

The scents of sterilized emergency rooms and newly dug graves fail
    to permanently leave my system.

Clammy handholds followed by firmly pressed prayers consume my
    days and haunt my nights.

Your self-destructive ways are now less "self".

You've curated wounds.

You've cloaked my pillows with tears.

You've allowed my fear to fester.

Turquoise Staircase

I no longer can feel your hugs.
Your wings wrap me tight.
You're a star across my sky,
my angel, my radiant light.

I feel you smiling down
from your turquoise staircase,
so I keep
climbin,
n' reachin
n' turnin up to you.

Eventually we'll be together.
The sun no longer shines the same,
but your spirit gives me a brighter day.
Your love keeps my candle aflame.

I feel you smiling down
from your turquoise staircase,
so I keep
climbin,
n' reachin
n' turnin up to you.

Invisible Friend

My mystic companion has been with me for a while.

She tends to be silent, but, oh boy, does she have style.

Prancing and dancing upon these pages,

never shy or meek in any of my life stages,

she loves to start at a point and welcome a flow

in the best of times or in moments quite dark and low.

I don't know what I would do without my invisible friend.

She helps me clearly see the places I need to amend.

If I am acting whack or out of line,

she always steps up and takes the time.

Invisible she may be;

however, she's the realest of the real for me.

Life

My circle allows me to breathe and inhales right alongside me.
I am empowered by my past.
I stay true to the roots that brace me,
roots that hold me up.
Branches that strike the links that try to chain me,
fruit that bears the sweetness of my legacy.

birth

birth:

the start of life; the emergence of a new individual

My Birth

I asked the grand universe, *Why me?*
She answered, *Your light lies within.*
My purpose is cemented.
Heel, toe to my glory.
Curbed my doubts and fears.
I found my stride.
I walk with
ease and
peace.

Eat, Prey, Love

Familiar habits and features

Seems to be a genuine creature

Head up high, sweet type of vibe

Intimidation at a low, guard fully blown

Entered with two swipes on a Welcome

Leaving traces of dirt, particles left to flirt

Got comfy and cozy rapidly

Zipped in and zipped down

Sinking into the cushion comforted by touch

Throws thrown, pillows flattened

Manifesting insatiable highs

Claiming the territory of her thighs

The call of the wild growling aloud

Alert, stenched, and proud

Silence enters, as he freshens for the exit

Leaving her amazed and dazed

Desires blocked her why's

An immediate rush, outpouring of cries

Lipstick smeared, head buried

This attraction should've never been hurried

Spending time licking wounds

Saliva heavy, laced with regrets

When will she cease and forget

Love doesn't quickly come

It burrows and dwells

Maybe one day a creature will treat her well

The Curtains Are Closing

I'd rather be burned by Rick James' crack pipe
than to let my heart yearn for you.
We are the epitome of an unforsaken tune,
the kind that gives B.B. the blues.

You do more remixing of groupies
than focusing on the beat that brought us together.
The DJ tries to spin the record,
toxicity scratches the vinyl.

Humming through the pain.
Picking the tired strings.
Striking all the chords.
Reaching a screeching octave.

When you belt, *No way, you're never gonna shake me*
Ooh, darling, 'cause you'll always be my baby,
I convince myself the piano keys
were made for you and me.

We have the most twisted of interactions.
We get caught up in the rapture.
Make love till the early morn.
Hoping to reach the chorus on the same note.

But my alto isn't harmonizing with your baritone.
I try to go high when you go low.
My tears stop my voice from peaking.
I don't want this duet anymore.

Our music isn't vibrating on the air.
No one is requesting our love on the radio.
Please just go ahead and get on that Midnight Train.
I'm sure your Dream Girl awaits.

We don't need to put on this show.
Feel free to lip sync because I don't give a damn anymore.
My mic is dropped.
The curtains are closed.

All Women?

Women are intricately woven layers of fabric that create a dynamic tapestry.

Some threads are clear to the eye,

while others need to be plucked from a hidden view.

These threads are the vibrant strands of their identities bridging together,

yet at the same time, you do everything in your power to unravel and rework it

because it does not fit your vision.

Intense eyes and, interestingly enough, confident justifications of,

I don't see color

followed by cocky proclamations of,

Women's rights are human rights!

are hysterically mimicked like the unveiling of the latest Snapchat filter.

Virtual flowers and glowing streaks paint themselves over the reality of marginalization.

Historically, and today, it has largely been ...

Women of color whose Indigenous blood is tested and treated as a symptom of subordination. Their pigment is inserted as a clause for a contract for decreased opportunities and half the pay.

Told to seal their mouths and be grateful to the hand that feeds them.

Queer and lesbian women whose love and expression is weaponized as a terror to this nation's non-existent innocence.

Gaslit into believing that who they are is a choice to live a life in eternal damnation.

Non-Christian women are pushed down well before they kneel for their daily prayers.

Crucified to a cross they do not believe in.

Nailed for worshipping past Jesus.

Poor women who work their asses off on the daily to provide for their families work 3-4 minimum wage jobs because the powers that be refuse to enact a living wage.

The privilege to live is not guaranteed, so only women residing in the middle and above deserve benefits.

Sex workers who take advantage of the deviant patriarchy they masterfully ride,

hoping to close the gap by increasing the span of their legs.

For once, putting cis men on their back, showing the world that they are capable of domination.

Women with disabilities who constantly advocate for their needs because those with able bodies fail to realize accommodations are not a hassle.

Ramps and mental health supports are necessary, but it's the tip of their iceberg whose existence needs exploring.

All of these women and their lived experiences have been outright excluded from the attention and gains of mainstream feminism.

Aren't they women?

Aren't they deserving of equity?

Shouldn't you be fighting for their liberation?

Is it all women you care for?

Or do you only look after the women

who look like you,

who act like you,

and believe sitting next to the White man is the crescendo?

The Root of the Problem

My hair plays a pivotal role in who I am as a woman.
I recognize that hair and physical attributes shouldn't be the foundational building block of identity, but for just a second or two, allow my hair to tell an all-too-real truth as to what makes me, me.

My hand will not shake you quite as much as the visual touch of my curls.
My black pigmented curls coiled around sunlight on a warm day are mesmerizing,
yet highly misunderstood at the same time.
The misunderstandings blend and create a synthetic identifier for me.

Here are my truths in an effort to retract the conjured up label:
Like clock-work, my strands are consistently stimulated by the intertwining chemistry of my Italian, French, and Black genes.
These strands have been gawked at, murmured about, and even touched without permission.

White women are quick to define and twist my locks to meet their narrow-minded expectations. Immediate suggestions and advice are thrown my way in an attempt to help a "sista" out.

Instead of asserting my frizz, in fear of being labeled as "untameably" Black,
I have allowed products to seep through and cover my layers.
For far too long, I hid my shine and volume behind mass-produced tools solely designed to force me to conform and straighten up.

Heat, chemicals, and tears all married together
as the extreme vow in hopes of being endorsed to enter a club—
a club I, for years, was wracking my brain trying to decipher the passcode for.

One quarter-size of product,

    three hours of straightening,

        scrambled silk caps,

            cosign or two.

My hair is craving nutrients that will activate growth and strength,
not the dual-purpose spray you all have miserably failed in bottling as solidarity.
Your voice and activism take a pause when your personal experience doesn't directly match up to an intersectional cause.
The minutes, hours, and days I spent obsessing and frequently altering my mane is an internally oppressive pool that I no longer desire to wade in.
I am more than down to escape the heat and dwell in the coolness under my crown,
a crown uniquely provided to me and freely worn for all to see.

I have had to defend my unapologetic tresses,
but I appreciate you taking the time to listen and not make ignorant guesses.
The next time around, we will both openly share
and truly get to the root of each other's hair.

Bloodline by Professor James Douglas Banks (aka my Dad)

Inside the land of 10,000 lakes,
the earth has moved, the earth has shaked,
bullets have flown, necks have been broken.
A courtroom is a vigil of judicial tokens.
400 years of tears and pain,
bloodlines broken again and again.
A Glock and a taser are two different weapons.
Unarmed men can make policemen feel threatened,
yet the streets never seem to change.
Minds must be taught, biases rearranged.
400 years of tears and pain,
bloodlines broken again and again.
Emotional releases were shared by the people.
Prayers and hymns were heard from church steeples.
A verdict was read, a decision given.
Jurors were in legislative precision.
400 years of tears and pain,
bloodlines broken again and again.
Change moves slowly when power is confronted.
Movements of equality cannot be blunted.
Continue to let your voices be heard,
work for peace, spread the word.
400 years of tears and pain,
bloodlines broken again and again.

Another Black Boy Gone

Just because that's how it's always been, doesn't mean it's business as usual.
This isn't a healthy habit.
This is a suffocation of my airway,
blood trickling down my trachea of those lost,
choking on the pain,
stabbed by grief, and
drowning in the sobs that go unanswered.

Called out,
pressed the keys and
heard a dial tone
without a sign of a ring, a glimpse of hope for connection.
So I screamed, pushed my head out of the window screeching out for help.

Hell, on Earth

You sneered, walked me into a glass-encased room,
sat me down and mimicked the charm of Satan himself.
Curled your blonde tail and gripped your trident.
Looked me in the eyes and proceeded to turn the heat up.

Used our weekly meeting as a recurring opportunity to check me,
force me into a box that you salivated at the mouth to mark.
Threw stones knowing that if I ducked or dodged
it would be a permanent account on my record.

My outcries and tears outline the illusions you have constructed.
Your savior-themed exhibit is nauseating.
Pictures of students are plastered on your walls as trophies
knowing damn well their gaps in learning aren't a prize to be won.

Images of coffee-rich girls are projected, applauded for being vocal,
and behind closed doors are told to obey the hand that feeds them.
Midnight-kissed boys are met with fearful eyes and harsh
punishment because their intelligence is intimidating.

Archetypal displays of heroes are put on a pedestal
even though they bash the community.
Had a mighty "S" on their chest
and put an end to our youth capitalizing on their skills.

Every time I attempted to pull out my paintbrush,
to blend the ink,
to make sense of the canvas,
you gaslit me into believing I was filling in the lines with

unnecessary strokes.

Chuckled when I said I am committed to showing my work.
Changed the subject when I said this institution is closing doors
and ignoring the rings of our families.
But it is you.

You are the problem.
You are the constant in this flawed mural.
Education is your playground.
The blue-eyed devil is you.

If You Really Wanna Know

I wasn't feeling it the second my alarm rang,

buzzing sound seething in my ears.

left to right, right to left.

My peace being the victim of theft.

Time lost to dwell and sit in front of this screen.

Staring intently into the black, wondering if I should muster and power on.

I wasn't feeling it.

I wasn't feeling it when my teacher said good morning,

yet all I could think of was mourning.

I am here, yet my grandfather is 6 feet beneath

while I am forcibly grinning through my teeth.

I wasn't feeling it when I had to answer endless questions with a click,

knowing my familial clique was forever out of order.

Distracted by the urge to place the memories in line.

Man, I wish he were present.

Craving his guidance that is oh-so pleasant.

Gramps lifting me on his lap to tickle the keys.

Third Wednesdays we filled the air with flair.

A chuckle here, a spin there.

Now it's mute upon entry, please beware.

I wasn't feeling it, but no one made a peep.

Not one person zoomed over while this little Black boy forcibly held back his weep.

I wasn't feeling it.

I tried, I tried to feel.

I tried to log in, push through, submit this and accept that,

but I am tired. My battery has slowly depleted.

I am not feeling it.

Zooming with a Gen Z

"When I was your age..."
I was a string bean with a polka dot face,
disappeared into my hoodie, only sprawled out for familiar friends,
crossed the street from hulky foes.

                You hide your face, shielding it from anyone to see.
           Filters aren't an available feature in your virtual classroom.

"When I was your age..."
I'd enter class with sincere boredom from reciting facts,
wrapped my two digits and thumb around my wooden tool,
chiseled away, doodled my escape until half past any period.

You wait for the host to start the meeting, hoping your Wi-Fi trips up
                and the lack of peer connection doesn't present itself.

"When I was your age..."
A pencil and pad were all I needed to dream.
Played MASH, strategically tallying and pinpointing my future:
veterinarian, four kids, Will Smith, mansion.

                Your world view is at the mercy of influencers and reposts.
                    TikTok outlines your next move and obsession.

"When I was your age..."
I prayed for my own version of Ferris Bueller's Day Off.
I couldn't have imagined being forced to stay home.
I only see the toll it would've taken on my sanity and health.

You have a blacked out screen, muted mic, and unread messages.
Your hope isn't piqued.

So you sit...sit and stare...stare and sit.

You aren't inspired to dream.
You aren't motivated to escape.
You are numb.

The "Up-and-Coming" Area

Livin' the dream

Repurposed paradise

Palm trees

Paved pathways

Hiked fees

Won't you be my neighbor?

Nah "G"

Keepin' it legit

Not sugar free

Mango cups, Tajin

Please no dopamine

Amenities overpriced

Ancestral hopes and

unrelenting tropes

perfectly spliced

So I...

I press my ten toes across the concrete
slabs of gray that echo a man's directorial cues

smile beautiful...
two words that crowd me

the nice guy mansplains his way across the asphalt
making an ass of himself, trying to make the queasy feeling my fault

so I smirk

my smirk

my teeth stay hidden
kicking it

hibernating in the dark
storing away my bliss

a pressure mounts for me to smile
a slight smile, not too much, not too little

an imbalance of sorts
where the top competes with the floor

just enough to mask disgust
enough to keep the questions at bay

if it wasn't for the roof
the cards of my house would reveal an angst

bubbling over like the sauces my foremothers
boiled to cleanse the acidic wishes of men

so I smirk

my smirk

an uneven yet perfectly placed act of rebellion
a spitting image of my lineage

lined with self-assurance
filled with gloss acting as a mirror of misogyny

glances shoot from the irises of my harasser
a darkness pools in his pupils

I push my smirk as an act of warfare
disarming the patriarchy

maiming the pimp hand
he thinks is strong

his tongue wagging stops
the head nods stiffen up

he waves his white flag
with his tail between his legs

so I smirk

my smirk

my mouth folds
cheer is reborn

uptick in the corners
blush pinks creased in relief

the cupid's bow of my lips
pucker up for time well lost

my smirk is a novel of some sorts
indents of tissue tell an esoteric story

it knows a secret
I am the daughter reborn

correcting misdirected karma
challenging fairytales

pushing against a cage
forcing the perils of men to dry out and chap

so I smirk

my smirk

Self-Checkout Isn't an Option

You pompously snatched the dollars from Grandma Jean's coin purse.
At the same time refused to dish out a fair wage to her granddaughter.
You rushed to encourage Reggie to buy 2-for-1 packs of chicken
while steady beefin' with his face-tatted nephew, who in your words looks "suspicious."

You enticed our people with a dangling carrot of opportunities,
simultaneously silenced their status as essential workers,
dismissed the heartbeat at the corner of Slauson and Crenshaw,
ignored the value of our being because it didn't increase your stock.

For decades you have presented as a staple on our block.
In reality fleeting greetings and flirtatious deals masked the fact that you couldn't care less about saving our lives.

Our neighborhood watch oversaw aisles and checked out our needs,
scanned our desires from the conveyor belt,
put themselves at risk to being engulfed by the spawns belted out by a deadly virus for us.

You pushed produce and healthy options
then turned around and hijacked the hood of a decent living,
maxed out the radius beyond a diameter our feet can travel.

We struggled to pull at your heart strings.
When we reached our hands for a tug,
you struck us with your Franklin-filled fists.

You now invite a food desert whose sand will simply blow across the parking lot,
dusting over our access to wellness.

You may have dried out our fluid access,
but our cup runneth over.

Self-checkout isn't an option.

Us Not Vs.

There is power in being surrounded by people that look like you,
to stare across tables, beyond playgrounds, in seats of influence and
view kind eyes, layers upon skin
that rival the rich soil that we were shipped from.

Stolen or fled, we lost the security of our lands,
forced to explore a new territory and comb fields,
placed in positions to scratch and claw beyond submission,
use our ingenuity to make a home for years to come.

To not know our origin,
but see coordinates of love and kinship is a blessing.
We are all in search of our lineage, our intersections of connection.
We do not want to look under rugs for the crumbs of affiliation.

We are Brown and Black siblings risen from the earth.
Aunties, uncles, abuelos, abuelas insert themselves
in a newly formed village since theirs were pillaged.
We are in community with one another.

Our native tongues are compromised
with the White plains of this land.
Oil palm ironically used to cleanse our mouths,
as languages are looked to be erased.

But our dialect of community enables us
to hear one another loud and clear.
Accents and vernacular are the means in which we bud from the
tongues of our ancestors.

Backed by the spirit of our relatives,
seasoned with culture,
spiced with pride,
stirred into finding a way to survive.

We rise before and after the dust settles.
Particles of manipulation and stereotypes do not taint our bonds.
The pressures of assimilation encouraged us to unite,
a daily reminder that we are stronger together.

Battle Cry

Ants go marching one by one, hurrah, hurrah.
The ants go marching one by one, hurrah, hurrah.
The ants go marching on by one,
the little one stops to scream, "We are far from done!" And they all go marching down to the ground.

Boom, boom, boom!

Skies stream the tears of mothers whose sons lay still.
Clouds erupt with the thunderous agony of Alton and Philando's daughters.

What would life be if we were like ants?
Microscopic beings ducking and dodging an inevitable downpour.

Frantically communicating to prevent their loves from being washed away. Transmitting messages of a surefire path to survival.

But Glorious Beings, we march because our Ancestors' tongues were ripped from their mouths. Fed lies and a narrative of inferiority despite the magic that nestled under their ribs.

Ants go marching two by two, hurrah, hurrah.
The ants go marching two by two, hurrah, hurrah.
The ants go marching two by two,
the little one stops to link arms with the crew and they all go marching down to the ground.

Boom, boom, boom!

Flowers saturated with coagulated blood of children long lost.
Tamir and Aiyana's petals were robbed of a full bloom, left to decay before peak season.

What would life be if we were like ants?
Microscopic beings on a fast track to syrupped scents.

In the pursuit of plush blueberries rolled onto our Earth's soil.
Salivating, leaving a trail for friends to feast.

But Glorious Beings, we protest because we are deprived of sweet justice. Our bitter taste reacts to poison-laden seeds planted in our community.

Ants go marching three by three, hurrah, hurrah.
The ants going marching three by three, hurrah, hurrah.
The ants go marching three by three,
the little one stops to mask the tear gas that's free and they all go marching down to the ground.

Boom, boom, boom!

Soil shakes as Eric's lungs collapse.
Pebbles bounce as Freddie's spine crumbles.

What would life be if we were like ants?
Microscopic beings who wait for proverbial orders from the top.

But Glorious Beings, we embody our Elders and tread with tenacity.
Engrave our shields with the names of those slain, repelling the rubber bullets of blue evil.

Ants go marching four by four, hurrah, hurrah.
The ants going marching four by four, hurrah, hurrah.
The ants go marching four by four,
the little one stops to recruit many more
and they all go marching down to the ground.

Boom, boom, boom!

Roots coil as Tony's life's grasped and their brethren stay silent.
Twisted roots whose hairs reclude as Roxanne's murder was covered due to her "choice".

What would life be if we were like ants?
Microscopic beings whose differences are stamped by rank.

But Glorious Beings, we must chant to honor the small footprints of kin who have big shoes to fill. Our voices must buoy to the changing waves of our deep waters.

We must part the seas to defend our bloodline.
We must share the coordinates of our sanctuaries for fellowship.

Ants go marching five by five, hurrah, hurrah.
The ants go marching five by five, hurrah, hurrah.
The ants go marching five by five,
the little one stops to fight to stay alive
and they all go marching down to the ground.

Boom, boom, boom!

We shall live in possibility. We shall march on.

Truth Be Told

I hear my calling.

Even when I am
disturbed,
discredited,
and downtrodden,
the voices lingering within will not die down.

I listen to the aspirations of our youth.
I meditate to the knowledge of our elders.
I chant the cries of our people.

My belief in my purpose changed the indent of my steps.
My prints are outlined with service and filled with the wealth of my community.

growth

growth:
a stage or condition in increasing, developing, or maturing

My Growth

I rub my back, wide with learned lessons.
I stroke my legs for standing firm.
Clap my hands to combat noise.
Drink tears of cynics.
Swallow milestones
for breakfast,
lunch, and
dinner.

This New Year

From the ciudad where lost angels flock,
to the depths of the Land of the Gods
where serenity dwells,
humanity scoured sunken sands and digital footprints for answers.

When the powers that be
turned a deaf ear to our entreaties,
we cajoled our inner voice,
and tricked our heart's vocation
into believing we can.

Prayers kissed fingertips in the moonlight,
pleas burrowed in the indents atop our knees,
our will surpassed the shallow sweat pools in the folds of our skin,
and we stood firm in the marigold rays of each day.

We drop the year behind us,
at the peak of fireworks,
we fling our goals
against the sky's dark sea, flowers of desire, and love's fervency.

May the hopes of our children seep in,
their innocence wraps our broken bones,
the warmth of their hugs heals our aches,
and their glee in the mundane
bubble up pastimes.

As moments of love, tussles of adventures,
barrels of laughs fill our eyes
our kin dry our cheeks,
our unbridled future shall hereditarily liberate us from our grief.

Flares guide a fresh start,
releasing the suffering at the hands of our egos,
so promises can spring true like shooting stars to make amends to thy neighbors.

Accountability will permeate the air,
kindness will pervade our airways,
we shall go beyond cups of sugar
and gifted arbugines from gardens
as an act of community.

Each new moon will usher in redemption
and permit our evenings to close as brethren,
we will harvest the urgency for altruism
where our consciousness is critical,
and our valor is unwavering.

Bread and Butter

Our family wasn't lacking the chedda for fancy snacks and treats,
but I went through a phase craving basic slices and smooth toppings.
Sopped yellow creamy dreams on a wheat-filled, soft, non-toasted piece of bread.

A simple, low-maintenance way to establish my autonomy.
At any time I could untwist the bag, skip by the end piece to retrieve a fluffy square,
open the drawer and pull out a shiny butter knife, crease into the tub and *smear, baby smear!*

I was in heaven. Appetite appeased and independence solidified.
I did not need Mama and Pops to fulfill my needs.
I did not have to wait for another to fulfill my desires.

I outgrew my love of buttered bread, but the pride remained.
I started to listen to myself of what I liked,
began to perk my ears to what I wanted.

As a grown woman, I'm not going out of my way to munch on some carbs,
but I do ask myself the daily question,

What am I innately good at?

What gifts do I bring to this world?

What is my bread & butter?

Just like the butter the young me loved.

I want to rest,
be merry, and
open the tub to opportunities to spread my presence on Earth.

The Unwritten Oath

All Hail Educators,

The days we spend obsessing about upcoming deadlines and tasks.
Pitching half past each hour perfecting our delivery.
Overseeing young motivation, hoping to channel it into seasoned thinkers.

The evenings we spend consumed with thoughts of the health of our students,
counting the number of children whose well-being grazes beyond the number of sheep we use to fall asleep.

The weekends we dedicate to preparing for a fresh start come Monday,
beads of liquid emotion running past our temples with ideas,
foreheads creased with creativity.

The months we commit to giving our youth the justice that failed to develop for us,
hands racing across pages, ink-filled sheets
leaving a trail of tears and blurred lines of trauma.

The years we rack our brains waiting for our neurons to transit information,
signalling potential solutions in dismantling this oppressive system's foundation,
passionate about creating a crack or two that can eliminate this cycle.

We are activists who use our speech and intellect to change the social fabric that is suffocating our kids.
Cotton that for centuries was picked from our kinfolk is sewn as textiles to confuse our Black and Brown babies from knowing the tapestry of their history.

Pressures attempt to mold and force us into curling up into a ball.

Our heads do not bow.
Our eyes do not cower.
Our hearts pump in unison with the families we are brought to serve.
Our backs remain strong, pressed into the spine of our ancestors.
Our shoulders are lifted by the joy our young leaders bring to a room.

If not us, then who?

We are not deterred by the challenge.
We empty the coins in our pocket.
We sacrifice the time with loved ones.
We dig into our heels because we know if we do not stand strong, our youth will be left to the devices of our nation.

Out of Office, into Living

The thrash of productivity,
the ring of announcements,
the blast of notifications bombard you
before you can even wipe the crust from the cradle of your eyes.

The 9-to-5 grind has sneakily evolved you into
a 13-hour professional monster.
You shouldn't have to slay these hours to stand atop of your castle,
so sit your booty down and listen to your heart.

Give yourself comfort.
Swaddle your energy.
Sink into the plushness of your essence
and cozy up to your spirit.

Bask in the company of your beauty
and experience the luxury of you.
Indulge in the presence of your being
to quiet the demands and expectations.

Preserve and jar the magic within you
to save the bottle of your fruit.
Limit the access of your sweet nature
so the world can't gobble you the fuck up.

Keep the array of your self-care intact.
Organize the boundaries that support your lines of sanity.
Fill in the columns with bliss.
Etch your rows with affirmations,

lines of messages that speak power unto you.
Let positive notes roll off your tongue
more than the hateful,
invalid syllables you utter when you are exhausted.

Prioritizing your health is more than self-love.
You are showing the world that you deserve to live.

Your feet are worthy of pressing into sandy beaches,
not solely for running errands for the office.

Your fingers deserve to tickle ivories and deliver vibrant notes,
not feverishly push keys for their weekly report.

Your nose should smell the scents of savory meals from distant lands,
not to sniff out the bullshit a company has mandated.

Resurrect your desires and allow yourself to dream.

Imagine an existence where you do not live to work,

a reality where your rest is necessary
and your experiences revolve around you.

Medicine Woman

Mother Nature, thank you for providing for me,
for restoring my belief in your charm.
The crisp mornings we share are my daily routine for sanity.
Your voice on my breeze enchants me.

The panoramic view of your bounty
captivates me with your offering.
I drink from the mouth of your rivers,
reveling in the sparkling waters of your mountains.

I am fueled by the vast sprouts in your fields.
The dew upon your leaves quenches my thirst for change.
Your blossoms nourish me from within &
heal my ill ways & tortured body.

Vitamins soak into my midsection,
eliminating my need to stomach the pains of society.
Your herbs shock the nerves out of my system,
putting me at ease with the confidence of your sturdy branches.

Your roots release splashes of the rainbow even after the rain remains.
Deep purples & reds spatter across the ground *beeting* sadness away.
Flower buds of emeralds skirt across my shins.
Canary yellows help me digest the pain humankind enacts.

Your kaleidoscope of brilliance peers through the shadows.
I am grateful for your generosity,
the unconditional love you give unto me.
There would be no me without you.

May I Have This Dance?

The sun begins to peek over and give a wink.
Skin feels the warmth of the playful keys.
The newborn day reaching its arms right around my waist,
ready to sashay and dip me into a fresh lesson.

> Hands pressing firmly into my flesh,
> guiding me out of my choppy steps,
> letting me weigh the pros of a groove,
> easily conning me into a harmonious duo.

The flirtatious start has me on the floor
while the vibrations are feeling me out
and filling me up,
spinning me to and fro.

> Edge of my lips stretch to raise the roof of my smile.
> Laughter permeating the air,
> taking my mind off of the melancholy tune
> that skipped mere hours ago.

No wallflowers here, just teeth standing loudly,
giving less than a damn about the old black record.
Day, take my hand and twirl me round.
Let these spectators relish in what we are all about.

Fly a Kite

Live to the height that your lungs can expand.
Let in glee, exhale pain.
Lift up into the sky so your strength is buoyant.
Float across robin's-egg-blue backdrops.
Be cushioned by comfy clouds.
Soar to your heart's content.
Used to run and hide,
now you can sprint into joy
past the finish line.
Leave trauma behind.
Soar, baby, soar!
Flip your shield into a fabric of dreams
that crease with air pockets of hope.

Your Ass is Grass

In the Spring...

I am green with positivity.
I lean to your rays.
Gleefully soak up the vitamin D
as nutrients burrow.

In the Summer...

I am lush with naivety.
My limbs willingly stretch out.
They grow with abundance,
eagerly awaiting to blossom.

In the Fall...

I am your stability,
a soft place to land,
your safe haven after work,
the scapegoat for your stains.

In the Winter...

I am your irritation.
I wrap you with my morning
brittle edges.
Every eve my blades nick more than skin.

THE Moment

There comes a moment in a woman's life
where she stirs an insurrection,
owns the destruction of years long past,
and releases stress as rubble silences the cries of her younger self.

There comes the moment in a woman's life
where she refuses to entertain fuckboys,
chuckles at the multiple nudes infiltrating her dms,
uses her mouth to roast men who seek to feast on her best.

There comes the moment in a woman's life
where she is enclosed by the love of her sisters who bunker down
into the capsules of her lungs,
so she can exhale the pressures on her shoulders.

There comes the moment in a woman's life
where a tango curates her physical solidarity.
Her feet roar in sync with her own 8-count
and she trusts her missteps to lead her way out of a frantic tune.

There comes the moment in a woman's life
where she gives the Benjamins the middle finger as her purpose
crawls out of a hole
and saunters in the sun whilst groundhogs dwell in the shadows.

This is the moment in a woman's life
where all the peaks and valleys come to fault line the lessons,
shake up her surface,
and settle her soul.

This is the moment in a woman's life
where she is in control of her horizon.
Her dreams dance with the clouds,
and her desires nestle in the feathers of her wingspan.

Royalty

Crown standing abundantly high,
the springboard of my regality.
Twisted strands are the playground for my brain waves.
Thoughts turned to hope
turned to elevated pathways,
flying leaps and bounds with the flutter of my angelic wings.
I hold fast to my untamed dreams,
for my dreams live like a fully-winged bird who gladly glides.
I have emerged...

My Favorite Two-Piece

This is an ode to the architect of my legacy,
the voluptuous foundation for my statuesque presence

Spectators attempt to be aficionados
Thinking they are at arm's reach when in reality
they are in the boondocks, miles away from locating my glory

Speckled with love dimples that blossom across the fields of my skin
Sending the sun to shimmy and shake
within each tender indent

They get jiggy with it and bounce at the sound of an 808
Salivating to battle any b-boy
Steadily earning the title of undefeated

The depths of my thighs exude care and generosity
Nestle and warm the ears of men in the depths of winter's climax
Making a place they wish to call home

The crescendo of my legs carries my body
across the roughest of terrains
Guiding each new step with a harmonious impact

Even when my feet are tired and mind is weary, my sturdy loins
muster up the strength to keep me going
Embracing the imprint I stamped along the way

My thighs stretch my mountain taller so that my ancestors can challenge the horizon
Reminding me to honor my matriarchy

This is a written promise note
I will love and honor every inch of my thick, melanated gift

This is an ode to the architect of my legacy
The voluptuous foundation for my statuesque present
This is an ode to my thighs

Do Not Disturb

Turn off the lights. Light a candle.
'Tis the night for solo handles.

I'm not looking for Pendergrass.
No soundtrack for my master class.

Recline, let thy fingers caress.
Pleasure I willingly harness.

Brimming lips absolutely parched.
Feet longing to buckle and arch.

Thigh brows smirking at the ceiling.
Back pressed, goosebumps a reeling.

Skimming the grounds of my estate.
Tips figuring an eight, gyrate.

Blind to all of the worldly woes.
Breathing hard as warmth spreads down low.

I trace the well of my being.
Skirting up, to and fro, freeing.

The dawn glistens upon my peak.
Golden hues run, dashing to streak.

Indulging in my coffee flesh.
Pulsating, hmmm self-possessed.

Slumber Soldier

I grace your sheets and wait for the opportune time to emerge.
I'll hurdle into your REM cycle, waddle into your dreams, and
burrow in your eccentric brain waves.

It's my honor to protect you in the depth of sleep.
To wade in the banks of your haunting memories.
To strip your pillows of sweat and eliminate the cases of stress.

Trust me to keep the ripple effect from seeping
into your lived experiences.
I shall be your slumber soldier slashing the demons of your mistakes.

Your intergalactic soul is home here.
Safety is well known here.
Serving you in the comfort of your bed is my honor.

I'll compress your fears into submission
and swaddle your inner child so it leaps with glee.
Your peace is such a moon when it's full.

I Take the Reins

I am the leader of my own destiny.
Wrong or right, my decisions are what rule.

I take
responsibility,
names,
control.

I am a
mover,
shaker,
moneymaker.

I am not a
follower,
lamb,
nor joke.

My position is high, and my purpose is almighty.
I take the reins.

Universe as I See It

I do not make myself digestible for the world.
You can choke on my celestial body.
My stellar ideas will not be nibbled down for your consumption.
You cannot wash me down with meteor showers.
Like a comet, my fortitude increases in energy.
You may orbit around my being, but this is not your space.

Acknowledgements

I dedicate this book to my loved ones. My circle of love that continues to surround me with care, support, and productive pushes when I am too stubborn or hardheaded to see my path.

To my parents who from a young age instilled the love of art and poetry in me by exposing me to Langston Hughes, Maya Angelou, and Gil Scott-Heron. My mother bombarded me with Motown and oldies while my father uplifted quiet spaces with the sounds of jazz and blues. Thank you both for helping the little girl in me learn from your experiences and find ways to soothe my soul when insecurities, doubt, and heartache came knocking at my door. More importantly, thank you for being the biggest cheerleaders and for the endless sacrifices you both made to show up and show out for your baby girl. It does not go unnoticed, and I am damn lucky to have you both guiding me and holding me up in my own personal journey.

To the students, families, and educators that I have partnered with over the years, thank you for trusting me as a teammate in our work for change. You inspired me and continue to light a fire under me to be a social justice leader who puts community liberation at the forefront. I feel extremely blessed to be alongside you and to witness you all step into your own purposes and gifts.

Last but not least, thank you to my sisters who the universe brought into my life. You all have wrapped your arms around me and have enclosed me with your love, wisdom and light. Thank you for reminding me daily of what it means to be a strong woman and leader.

About the Author

Jasmine Banks is a career educator, encourager, and self-proclaimed thought partner. Growing up, she struggled with confidence and feared being acknowledged by others. She did not want attention nor did she want to even be noticed. Looking back, she realized that she actually feared people boxing her in by shaping her into the negative and ugly mold of a stereotypical Black woman. As a young woman, it was rare to see BIPOC, especially women of color, portrayed positively in the media. Despite having powerful role models and images in her family and community, she internalized these implicit messages and in turn silenced herself and dulled her shine.

Becoming an educator is what tipped the scale to proclaiming that enough is enough and to finally embrace her power from within. She could not look at herself in the mirror and encourage students and adults to be unapologetic, when at the end of the day she was tossing and turning in bed with self-critiques and questions of "Am I good enough?", "I won't be heard anyways.", and "You aren't ready.", to name a few. Yes, we all have insecurities and at times little moments of doubt, but the difference is letting the doubt overshadow the shine.

Every day she makes a choice. A choice to make a priority to investing in herself and her community. Her purpose in life is to encourage other BIPOC to do the same for themselves through her servitude, actions, and ultimately with her shared personal journey of self-love and empowerment in this book.

Jasmine resides and leads in South Los Angeles. In her free time, Jasmine enjoys basking in nature, writing, spending time with loved ones, and taking on rigorous physical challenges.

Thank you for reading the story inside of me. I hope this encourages you to unapologetically speak your truth and allow the world to revel in the story inside of you.

Made in the USA
Las Vegas, NV
10 August 2023